PRAYERS
&
PETITIONS
FOR MY
cancer
WARRIOR

WORDS TO PRAY WHEN YOU
DON'T KNOW WHAT TO SAY

by

YVETTE PERRIER QUANTZ, RDN, LDN

IN LOVING MEMORY OF:

Marie Adele Diano-Arbour (maternal grandmother),

1982 breast cancer Warrior.

Jeanne Marie Arbour (godmother),

1983 throat cancer Warrior.

Laura Lee Webre-Perrier (paternal grandmother),

1998 lung cancer Warrior.

Dr. Michael Robert McElderry (uncle),

2019 skin cancer Warrior.

CONTENTS

"cancer doesn't deserve a capital c."

— Cheryl Arbour

ACKNOWLEDGMENTS

Don't thank me. Thank God.

—Mrs. Clara Bell, also known as Mama Bell or MaBell, who as I write this is 99 years old, still thanking God for today. From my earliest memories, she taught me to always thank God first.

I'll start there.

Thank You, God.

Thank You for the people, experiences, time, and courage to share these words with others walking with their cancer Warrior.

Thank You for using me as Your instrument.

For years You've been asking me to write and share the words You've given me. For years I've been trying to run or hide from this calling.

Thank You for your patience and persistence.

Thank You for opening my stubborn heart and giving me the strength to listen and follow Your call.

I now know this book is only the beginning of future words to be shared, and since I couldn't begin to thank everyone who's been part of this journey, I'll start with You.

Thank You, God, for making this work possible.

PREFACE

This isn't a book I wanted to write, and I imagine it's not a book you want to read. You're here because someone you know has been diagnosed with cancer, and you want to pray it away. I get it.

If I could, I'd promise these prayers will cure everything. Unfortunately, that's not how cancer works.

In 2017, after learning my uncle John, my father-in-law, and a dear friend all had cancer, the words "You're in my thoughts and prayers" were said almost as casually as "Hello." While I didn't like this canned response, it's all I knew to say. I felt like an imposter.

Despite being strong in my faith, I wasn't sure how to pray for someone other than adding their name to a list of prayer intentions. Every week during Sunday service, or anytime prompted to lift up special intentions, I'd always pray for my loved one battling cancer. However, those moments of pause were usually followed by a pang of guilt. Why wasn't I praying for them as frequently or intentionally as I wanted?

That's when I heard Him whisper, *You're not the only one who feels lost when praying for loved ones with cancer. What if you wrote prayers that could be shared? I'll help you.*

Since I'm neither an expert in praying nor a scholar in writing, I told Him to find a professional.

Ten months later, I received a call from my aunt Adele: "Uncle Mike has cancer—stage 4 melanoma." My stomach dropped as tears began to flow.

This wasn't supposed to happen.

Another whisper: *What about the prayer journal?*

Maybe, I silently replied.

Two months later, I received a call from my mom: "Aunt Cheryl has cancer." All I could do was look up and scream, *Are you kidding me?*

The voice was no longer a whisper. *Time to start writing.*

I cried in response, *When will I find the time? Why me? I'm not trained for this!*

Then I remembered that writing has always been my way of praying; it's how I talk to God. Saying prayers for my loved ones battling cancer was important to me. I knew that if I was going to pray with intention, I'd better start writing.

One evening, after bedtime prayers with my daughters, I heard the voice again: *Let's call it Prayers & Petitions for My cancer Warrior.* Something about the words "cancer Warrior" pulled me in.

Putting pen to paper, this book began. Unsure if or how I'd share these words with others, I knew I had to write them. Something important was being asked, and I couldn't ignore it any longer. It was time to trust Him and listen.

A few months later, during a visit with my uncle Mike, he shared, "I'm not angry with God. There is a reason for all of this ... I've seen so much goodness in people."

Before fear could silence me, I told him about these prayers I'd been writing. "I hope to share with others one day." The look on his face confirmed there was no turning back.

As I was finalizing this book, I received a call from my dad: "It's cancer." Again, I found myself questioning, *Why? Haven't we had enough? I can't do this!! He told me, Keep going. Your cancer Warrior needs you.*

INTRODUCTION

For as long as I can remember, writing prayers has been my way of connecting and conversing with our heavenly Father. I'm honored, humbled, and in all honesty, a little hesitant to share these prayers with you.

Honored because you're reading this, allowing me to walk on this journey with you and your Warrior.

Humbled because through God's love, strength, and grace, this book was published.

Hesitant because these are personal prayers, written during very private moments.

The truth is there's no right or wrong way to pray. Our Father knows what's in your heart, and He knows what tomorrow will bring. Lifting the name of a loved one brings spiritual blessings and strength to their soul.

On the following pages, you'll find prayers and petitions inspired by my cancer Warriors' journeys. Use them to facilitate your conversation with our Father. After each prayer, there's a page for personal journaling.

During the final days with my uncle, he said, "Never lose hope, have faith, and know God will always take care of you."

Now I share these words with you.

Don't lose hope.

Keep the faith.

Know your cancer Warrior needs you.

Your prayers and petitions matter.

In peace, love, and strength,

Yvette

P.S. Per my aunt, Cheryl Arbour: "cancer doesn't deserve a capital c." Therefore, you'll never see cancer capitalized in this book. If you know her, then you can appreciate that when she says something, you listen.

MY cANCER WARRIOR

The prayers and petitions of this book are dedicated to:

_____

_____

_____

_____

_____

Who is battling:

_____

_____

_____

_____

_____

Dear Lord,

May you give us the strength, wisdom, and courage to face each day covered in your armor and protection.

Amen

COLLECTION: *the*
PRAYERS
&
PETITIONS

THE DIAGNOSIS

Dear Lord,

I recently learned _____ was diagnosed with cancer. I'm sad and confused.

This wasn't supposed to happen.

It's never supposed to happen.

Yet it's happening.

I don't know what to do. I don't know what to say.

I want to help. I don't want to get in the way.

I come, asking You to wrap Your arms around Your cancer Warrior. Give Your peace and strength as this trial begins.

As _____ begins this journey, give the family, friends, medical team, and me the strength, courage, words, and wisdom to help.

Help us stay strong in our faith and trust that You have this.

Amen.

My cancer Warrior ...

_____
_____
_____
_____
_____
_____
_____
_____
_____
_____
_____
_____
_____
_____
_____
_____
_____
_____
_____

When I am afraid, I put my trust in you.

PSALM 56:3

PROCESSING THE NEWS

Heavenly Father,

As the news of this diagnosis sets in, more questions and concerns arise. It feels unfair as to why this is happening. It's hard to understand the purpose of this pain.

While processing this news, I recognize that talking about cancer feels scary and uncomfortable. I don't want my fear of saying the wrong thing or not knowing what to say to keep me from serving my Warrior.

I'm asking for Your help on this journey.

Give _____ the strength and courage to face each day.

May Your wisdom guide me in supporting _____. Please show me how to lean into uncomfortable situations or conversations so that I may help and serve.

May Your peace help us process the purpose of this pain.

Amen.

As this journey begins ...

_____

_____

_____

_____

_____

_____

_____

_____

_____

_____

_____

_____

_____

_____

_____

*Therefore put on the full armor of God, so that when the
day of evil comes, you may be able to stand your ground,
and after you have done everything, to stand.*

EPHESIANS 6:13

PRAYING FOR A MIRACLE

Dear God,

There are so many things I want to pray for; there's so much to ask. Healing, strength, peace, love, support, when, how, and why?

Why is this happening? Why now?

Yet here we are.

Can I ask for a miracle? Do I even believe in miracles?

Yes, I do. I'm going to ask You for a miracle.

I've heard of Your miracles before and I'm asking for one now.

Will You heal my cancer Warrior? Please?

There, I've put it out there. I want a miracle, the miracle of Your healing.

I want pre-cancer life back. I'll accept life's annoyances and frustrations, find the good, spread joy, and complain less. I promise.

Will You please perform a miracle and heal _____?

In You I trust.

Amen.

Heal my Warrior ...

Jesus looked at them and said, "With man this is impossible, but with God all things are possible."

MATTHEW 19:26

ASKING FOR A MIRACLE

Dear Lord,

I've experienced enough and understand that wishing cancer away or hoping it's a bad dream is living childlike, and I'm not a child anymore.

I've learned the miracles that happen are rarely the miracles for which I ask.

Still, I won't stop believing in miracles. I won't stop asking or praying for a miracle. However, I know that praying for a miracle probably won't make one happen.

What else can I do? I want to help. I want to fix things. Can You take it away? Can I ask that of You?

Loving God, I believe in Your miracles. If it is Your will to cure _____, I trust it will happen. If curing this cancer is not part Your plan, give us courage and strength to take the next step.

No matter what tomorrow may bring, I pray that You will open our eyes, hearts, and minds to the miracle of Your love.

Amen.

May we see the miracles ...

_So do not fear, for I am with you; do not be dismayed,
for I am your God. I will strengthen you and help you;
I will uphold you with my righteous right hand._

ISAIAH 41:10

IF NOT, THEN WHAT?

Eternal Spirit,

I come humbly before You, knowing there's more than a miracle to ask, beg, and pray.

There's much my Warrior, and the people who are surrounding _____will need during this battle with cancer. Most of these things are beyond my ability to do or deliver. What is needed most can only be achieved with Your grace and love.

Still, I don't want to be a bystander during this battle.

Reveal to me how I can help.

Guide me in Your ways.

Lead me in service.

Give me words of wisdom.

Direct my prayers and petitions.

Where can I bring peace, comfort, and joy?

Show me, guide me, lead me.

Amen.

Show me how to help ...

_____

_____

_____

_____

_____

_____

_____

_____

_____

_____

_____

_____

_____

_____

_____

_____

*And my God will meet all your needs according
to the riches of his glory in Christ Jesus.*

PHILIPPIANS 4:19

HEAVY HEART

Dear Lord,

I come to You with a heavy heart, as I'm still processing the news.

It doesn't make sense why _____ has to suffer. It's hard to understand why this is happening.

I know I'm not the only one sad and confused, and I ask for You to lift the burden of our heavy hearts.

As my Warrior begins this journey, give the mental and physical stamina for the most courageous fight.

Extend this braveness and strength to family, friends, the medical team, and myself.

Wrap Your arms around us as You bring peace and comfort, reminding us of Your everlasting love.

Amen.

When our hearts get heavy ...

"*Be strong and courageous. Do not be afraid or terrified because of them, for the LORD your God goes with you; he will never leave you nor forsake you.*"

DEUTERONOMY 31:6

FOR THE FAMILY

God Most High,

I bring my Warrior's family to You as they embark upon this journey.

Since the "c" word entered their lives, it seems things will never be the same.

I pray they will turn to You for strength to move forward each day.

When dark feelings of sadness, anger, hopelessness, or confusion take hold, may Your flame be their light.

Guide them with Your peace and love. Provide them with words to quiet their minds.

Let them not sit in silence out of worry or fear. Instead, give them courage for honest conversations.

Heal any wounds of the past, allowing them to move forward in forgiveness and love.

I lift up the family of _____, asking that they feel Your presence today and each day forward.

Amen.

Cover this family . . .

---

*"Do not let your hearts be troubled. You
believe in God; believe also in me."*

JOHN 14:1

FOR THE MEDICAL TEAM

Our Father, our Shield,

Protect and guide the medical team who is treating and caring for _____. Be with the doctors, nurses, lab techs, administration, and staff, along with anyone else who is part of this journey.

I bring them to You, asking You to deliver the strength, wisdom, and courage to do what is right. Give them what is needed to do their job.

Supply them with the energy necessary, both mentally and physically, for the work of their hands. When one of them needs to share news of hope or sadness, provide them with the words.

Give them patience and stamina as they make decisions and take action on what they are trained to do. Keep safe their minds, hearts, and hands, and bless all their families and friends as they treat and care for my Warrior.

Thank You for this medical team.

Amen.

Pray for them by name ...

---

*May the favor of the Lord our God rest on us; establish the work
of our hands for us – yes, establish the work of our hands.*

PSALM 90:17

REMOVE DISTRACTIONS

Teacher,

Help reduce and remove distractions and disturbances that may interfere with the treatment and care of my Warrior.

Take away any interruptions that are inessential to the health and healing of _____.

Present the family with insight into the unnecessary things that are occupying their days.

Allow the medical team to give their full attention to the work before them.

Let everyone remember that no matter the challenge, Your goodness and glory will prevail.

May all trust in You to provide what is needed to complete the work of Your will.

Protect the hands, hearts, and minds of everyone surrounding my Warrior during this time.

Amen.

For these distractions, I pray …

_____

_____

_____

_____

_____

_____

_____

_____

_____

_____

_____

_____

_____

_____

_____

_____

_____

"But as for you, be strong and do not give up,
for your work will be rewarded."

2 CHRONICLES 15:7

FOR THE MIND

God the Father,

I'm bringing You the mind that is set on overdrive thinking about the future. For when the mind starts to run, it can lead to scary and dangerous places.

Like a roller-coaster ride, thoughts can quickly move from being fearless to filled with anxiety and worry, causing one to stop living in the present and instead become consumed by what's next.

I know You can calm the storm and slow down the thoughts pouring through _____'s mind.

Hit the brakes to stop the overwhelming rush of fear from the unknown.

Quiet the mind and calm the voices.

Replace worry and fears with Your ever-present peace and all-encompassing love.

Bring rest and stillness.

Let us remember to trust You in all things.

Amen.

Calm the storm ...

---

*Do not be anxious about anything, but in every situation,
by prayer and petition, with thanksgiving, present your requests
to God. And the peace of God, which transcends all understanding,
will guard your hearts and your minds in Christ Jesus.*

PHILIPPIANS 4:6–7

RELIEVE THE SUFFERING

God,

I know my Warrior is suffering, both physically and emotionally. This pain makes it difficult and sometimes impossible to face each day.

I wish I could lessen the agony and take away the pain. I recognize I can't. Still, I ask of You: If there's another way to ease the discomfort, please show the way.

As human beings, we can get so set on doing things one way that we stop exploring other options. Sometimes our stubbornness keeps us stuck.

If there are other options to relieve the pain, lead the way.

If everything humanly possible is being done, may Your presence bring strength to endure the suffering on this journey.

Your love is stronger than any treatment or pill, and You have the power to heal. Please ease the pain and suffering of _____ today.

Amen.

Show me how ...

_____

_____

_____

_____

_____

_____

_____

_____

_____

_____

_____

_____

_____

_____

_____

_____

*Praise be to the God and Father of our Lord Jesus Christ,
the Father of compassion and the God of all comfort, who
comforts us in all our troubles, so that we can comfort those
in any trouble with the comfort we ourselves receive from God.*

2 CORINTHIANS 1:3–4

THANK YOU

My Lord, My Father,

I recognize I've been coming to You with prayers and petitions to take this away, work a miracle, and cure my Warrior. However, I realize I haven't taken the time to thank You.

My heart is sad to see the suffering, and there's still so much I want to ask of You. Yet, I'm reminded that there's much to be grateful.

Today I come with gratitude and thanksgiving.

For allowing me to experience the goodness.

For the lessons we've learned.

For the laughs we've shared.

For the tears we've shed.

For the joy and sorrow.

For the memories.

For this life.

For Your love.

Today, I simply thank You for _____.

Amen.

I'm grateful for how my Warrior ...

I will give thanks to you, Lord, with all my heart;
I will tell of all your wonderful deeds.

PSALM 9:1

FEAR OF MISSING OUT

My Heavenly Father,

Today I'm praying for my Warrior's feelings of the fear of missing out (FOMO). With so many other needs, it might seem odd to be praying for FOMO. However, the emotions surrounding the fear of missing out are real.

You designed us, Your children, in Your image and likeness. We're social beings who find joy in communion with others. And because of this, it's not uncommon to experience loneliness when unable to celebrate together.

For this, I'm seeking Your help.

Send your spirit to cover _____ with Your love and affection.

Flood the mind and heart of my Warrior with happy, joy-filled memories.

Remove all feelings of fear and despair.

Give us (friends and family) the insight and wisdom to share words that bring comfort, peace, hope, and joy.

Amen.

Send your spirit ...

May the God of hope fill you with all joy and peace as you trust in him,
so that you may overflow with hope by the power of the Holy Spirit.

ROMANS 15:13

FOR LONELINESS

Dear Jesus,

I'm here before You now, laying my Warrior's loneliness at your feet. I know being isolated is a struggle. I see the withdrawal and sadness in the eyes of my Warrior.

My company, even though appreciated, cannot fill the void this cancer has created.

You are the only One who can help.

Today, my prayer is simple: Bring comfort and peace to _____.

Let Your presence be known.

Protect the mind from negative thoughts, and guard the heart with Your armor.

When loneliness and despair want to take over, send Your love and peace to prevail.

Amen.

May Your love and peace ...

_____

_____

_____

_____

_____

_____

_____

_____

_____

_____

_____

_____

_____

_____

_____

_____

_____

_____

The Lord is my shepherd; I lack nothing.

PSALM 23:1

FOR THE PHYSICAL PAIN

God of all Grace,

My Warrior is hurting. The physical aches and pains of this disease are something I do not understand. While I cannot fully comprehend the extent of suffering, I see the distress and discomfort are real.

Today, I bring my Warrior's physical agony to You and ask for relief. May the pain not keep _____ from experiencing the gifts You've given.

Give me insight into how I can help comfort.

Please show me how to bring peace and relief.

Lead me with the wisdom of words and deeds to help.

Amen.

Bring comfort and relief ...

---

*But he said to me, "My grace is sufficient for you, for my power
is made perfect in weakness." Therefore I will boast all the more
gladly about my weaknesses, so that Christ's power may rest on me.*

2 CORINTHIANS 12:9

FOR FAITH

Eternal Spirit,

I understand that the faith inside of us comes from You. Our faith is not something we can see, feel, or touch. Yet it endures through the hardest of days.

When things become difficult and the pain unbearable, we may question our faith. Even the most faithful of Your servants are not beyond reproach; it's part of being human.

Today I pray for my Warrior's faith.

Restore it if it's weakened.

Resolve it if it's questioned.

Give the courage to share it with others.

Let faith in You be a guide and compass for others, especially those questioning why this is happening.

Strengthen _____'s faith today and each day moving forward.

Preserve our faith as we continue on this journey.

Amen.

Strengthen the faith ...

---

*I pray that out of his glorious riches he may strengthen
you with power through his Spirit in your inner being, so
that Christ may dwell in your hearts through faith.*

EPHESIANS 3:16–17

FOR ANGER

God of Peace,

I lay the feeling of anger at your feet.

"Anger" is such an ugly word. It's not something I like to associate my Warrior with, especially during this time. Still, it's a human emotion experienced by everyone at one time or another.

Just as cancer can spread and take over the body, so can anger take over the spirit. Without Your love and grace, anger can consume the soul, stealing the love and joy that was once there.

When anger takes hold, it is easy to forget about all the good things in life. Anger thrives on impatience, hatred, blame, and violence.

Anger turns the heart from You while stealing joy and depleting energy. Hate and anger do not heal; they only cause harm.

Today, I pray that the emotion of anger does not consume _____'s soul.

Amen.

May Your love and goodness ...

But you, Lord, are a compassionate and gracious God,
slow to anger, abounding in love and faithfulness.

PSALM 86:15

REPLACE THE ANGER

God of Heaven,

If there's anger in the heart of _____, I ask for Your grace to release it and to replace it with peace, love, and joy.

Perhaps the anger is directed at the cancer, or at a loved one, the medical team, or oneself. Only You and my Warrior will know.

Whatever the reason anger is present, replace it with forgiveness, acceptance, and harmony.

I ask You to help _____ walk in peace and understanding. If emotions of anger, impatience, frustration, resentment, or hatred visit, let them be brief and let them be teaching.

As these emotions pass through, may my prayers and encouragement bring comfort and peace. May my Warrior live in harmony, as You calm the storm.

Amen.

May my friendship bring ...

_____

_____

_____

_____

_____

_____

_____

_____

_____

_____

_____

_____

_____

_____

_____

Refrain from anger and turn from wrath;
do not fret—it leads only to evil.

PSALM 37:8

A PLEA FOR HELP

My Loving God,

Help _____ ...

Feel Your love over the hurt and pain.

Give thanks over condemnation.

Trust Your plan, rather than reside in doubt.

Discover joy over sorrow.

Experience peace in place of anger.

Depend on You in lieu of earthly desire.

Remain faithful in times of despair.

I place before You all the burdens weighing on _____'s heart.

I ask You to bring relief with Your peace and love.

Amen.

Help my Warrior ...

---

*I lift up my eyes to the mountains — where does my help
come from? My help comes from the L*ORD*, the Maker
of heaven and earth. He will not let your foot slip —
he who watches over you will not slumber.*

PSALM 121:1–4

FOR THE ROUGH DAYS

Father,

Today was a rough day. I'm tired, worn out, and in need of rest. I want this trial to be over. I pray tomorrow is better.

Thinking of my Warrior and all of the rough days, when nothing goes as it should and everything seems to go wrong. The times of questioning the purpose of this pain, the days I question You: those are the roughest of days.

Today I lift up my Warrior and ask that You replace the darkness with Your comfort, peace, and light.

Let the roughest of days be followed by better, brighter tomorrows. May Your strength carry my Warrior through.

Allow Your peace to bring rest to the mind, body, and soul.

May we always have hope, that even on the roughest days, a brighter tomorrow will prevail.

Amen.

When having a rough day ...

He heals the brokenhearted and binds up their wounds.

PSALM 147:3

FOR THE BETTER DAYS

Gracious Father,

Yesterday was rough. Today was a little better. It wasn't great; still, it wasn't terrible. I'm reminded to be grateful for the ordinary, not-so-awful days.

Thinking of my Warrior, I want to pray for better days.

Let ordinary things bring comfort and peace.

Allow _____ to experience joy from simple things in life.

Bring ease where there are challenges and patience where there are struggles.

May the better days be more frequent than the rough days.

Bless my Warrior with many more good days.

Give _____ peace of mind to recognize the goodness in this life when it is gifted.

Thank you for the better days.

Amen.

Thank you for the ordinary days ...

_____

_____

_____

_____

_____

_____

_____

_____

_____

_____

_____

_____

_____

_____

_____

_____

He says, "Be still, and know that I am God; I will be exalted
among the nations, I will be exalted in the earth."

PSALM 46:10

TRUSTING YOUR PLAN

My Lord,

It's no secret that this journey has been challenging, leaving much uncertainty and doubt.

Yet I know You have a plan.

I trust You have a plan.

Help us find the strength, courage, and peace to do what we need to do.

When we're tempted to plant seeds of fear, uncertainty, and doubt, let us turn to You.

Give us what's needed to nurture seeds of love, hope and peace.

Remind us to trust in You, in Your goodness, in Your love, and in Your plan.

Thank You for this day and all the blessings You have given.

Amen.

Help us trust Your plan ...

---

*My salvation and my honor depend on God; he is my mighty
rock, my refuge. Trust in him at all times, you people;
pour out your hearts to him, for God is our refuge.*

PSALM 62:7–8

SHOW US YOUR RAINBOW

Heavenly Father,

There's no hiding it—we're scared about what the future will hold for our Warrior. The truth is, once cancer has entered, life will never be the same.

I pray that we'll see the good in everyone. Give us peace in our hearts and with one another. Allow our peacefulness to comfort _____.

Help us remember that just because life has changed, this doesn't mean our days will be all bad or forever sad.

Let us see Your rainbow.

I know that even after the most brutal of storms, the most beautiful rainbows can appear. The beauty painted in the sky is always a reminder of Your power and glory.

Father, I ask: When we feel hopeless and lost in this storm, show us Your rainbow. And may we always remember this is a sign of Your covenant with all humankind.

Amen.

When I think of Your rainbows ...

"I have set my rainbow in the clouds, and it will be the sign of the covenant between me and the earth. Whenever I bring clouds over the earth and the rainbow appears in the clouds, I will remember my covenant between me and you and all living creatures of every kind."

GENESIS 9:13–15

FOR ANOTHER DAY

Loving God,

   I come to You with gratitude and thanksgiving.

   Thank You for:

   The conversation, tears, and laughter we've shared.

   Opening the heart to Your will.

   The strength and courage to share Your words.

   The desire to spread Your love.

   The gift of peace and forgiveness.

   Today, I want to simply say Thank You for another day with _____.

Amen.

For this day I thank you …

_____

_____

_____

_____

_____

_____

_____

_____

_____

_____

_____

_____

_____

_____

_____

_____

_____

*I always thank my God for you because of
his grace given you in Christ Jesus.*

1 CORINTHIANS 1:4

A TIME FOR REST

Dear Lord,

Send Your strength, grace, and goodness to help
_____ slow down, be patient, rest, and heal.

Rest allows healing to happen.

Yet the world has glorified the busy, the active, and the doers of the world. The truth is, society often celebrates cancer Warriors who don't let their battle with cancer slow them down.

Still, rest allows healing to happen.

Help my Warrior remember that there's a time for everything. There are things, no matter how many mind-over-matter mantras we recite, that won't be achieved until we learn to surrender and rest. Handing over the reins can be more challenging than trying to push through the discomfort.

Still, rest allows healing to happen.

If they're being called to rest, help my Warrior find peace in the stillness. If being called to move, give the strength and courage to take the next step.

Whatever is being asked, may we always trust You.

Amen.

Help my Warrior find peace ...

Then, because so many people were coming and going that they
did not even have a chance to eat, he said to them, "Come with
me by yourselves to a quiet place and get some rest."

MARK 6:31

THE RETURN OF CANCER

My God,

As You already know, the cancer is back. My Warrior is once again entering the physical and emotional journey of more tests and treatments.

I want to ask: How can this happen again? Yet I understand those answers are not for me to know.

Today I'm bringing this pain and suffering before You. Help _____ through this.

Give the medical team the knowledge and wisdom needed. Help the family as they re-enter this journey, and give them strength and courage to face each day.

If it's part of your will, can You give us more time? If yes, how much more time? Only you have this answer.

While our human hearts will always want more time, Your love and peace can prepare us for Your will.

Dear Lord, may Your mercy and grace be bestowed upon my Warrior during the treatment of cancer's return.

Amen.

Bestow Your grace and mercy ...

And the prayer offered in faith will make the sick person well;
the Lord will raise them up. If they have sinned, they will be forgiven.

JAMES 5:15

the GOLDEN COLLECTION: PRAYERS FROM MOTHER

THE TRUE CONSTANT

My mother, Yvonne Arbour Perrier, wrote the next collection of prayers. Aside from being my greatest teacher and best friend, she is also a beautiful writer. I hope her words and wisdom bring you comfort and peace. — Yvette

While composing these prayers, memories of my mother standing tall and erect during Mass services, bellowing songs coupled with congregational hymns, flooded my mind. A devoted wife and loving mother to her ten children (yes, you read that correctly!), prayer was the foundation of her life. My mother, bless her soul, escaped daily to her room for quiet prayer time. She prayed for peace and harmony along with our safety, education, spiritual nourishment, and health.

However, I wonder if she forgot to include herself in prayer. In 1981, when my mother was only fifty-six years old, I had to deliver the fatal news that all medical treatments were unsuccessful. She looked up at me from her hospital bed and responded, "Let thy will be done."

One year later, that nasty illness knocked on my family's door again and kidnapped my sister Jeanne. She was only twenty-eight years old at the time.

Today, while facing past, present, and potential future losses of loved ones to cancer, I find comfort in the practice of journaling my prayers, thoughts, and reflections.

I've outlived both my parents by at least ten years of age. I've grown wiser, calmer, less judgmental, and more realistic over these years. I hope my prayers contain words, thoughts, and insights about all this life has to offer and, more so, how death is a part of life. Death, while tragic, can also be experienced as a gift.

Treatments for cancer have changed profoundly over the past forty years. And today, a cancer diagnosis is not—and should not be—directly associated with death.

With all the changes and advancements that have evolved, prayer is the one thing that has remained a true constant.

I'm grateful for my life experiences, good and bad. I am thankful for my daughter, and I thank you, reader, for praying together for all of our cancer Warriors!

Yvonne

TRUST THE UNKNOWN

Light of the World,

Shine Your rays upon _____'s cancer diagnosis. Hold my Warrior's unsteady hand as the series of medical procedures confirm the presence of disease.

We, the shadows of Your light, pray for calmness, trust, and acceptance. The almighty powerful "Serenity Prayer" speaks these three profound words: *accept*, courage, and *wisdom*.

Wrap Your arms around my Warrior and all that awaits, affirms, and articulates the medical diagnosis.

Bless them with a heart to ACCEPT Your will.

Whisper COURAGE for the next steps.

Cover the minds of my Warrior and the medical teams with Your WISDOM.

Amen.

For courage and wisdom to accept ...

_____
_____
_____
_____
_____
_____
_____
_____
_____
_____
_____
_____
_____
_____
_____

*"I have told you these things, so that in me you may
have peace. In this world you will have trouble.
But take heart! I have overcome the world."*

JOHN 16:33

CALM THE STORM

My Lord,

Aid my Warrior's loved ones and teach them to live by the word *serenity* in a state of being calm, peaceful, and untroubled.

As You calmed the troubled waters, stilled the storm to a whisper, and hushed the raging waves of the sea, please guide all who face the storm that lies ahead. This storm will bluster into the lives and health of my Warrior's loved ones, at times leaving a wake of fury and rage.

Be gentle in testing their faith in You; they are strong loved ones of their Warrior.

Give them the strength, courage, and wisdom to cry out to You in times when they are sinking in fear.

Stretch out Your arms to enfold loved ones when panic strikes during this troubled time.

Let us all remember that You can calm this storm.

Amen.

When entering troubled waters . . .

Whoever dwells in the shelter of the Most High will rest in
the shadow of the Almighty. I will say of the LORD, "He is
my refuge and my fortress, my God, in whom I trust."

PSALM 91:1–2

63

DEFEND THE BODY

Mighty One,

Please help _____accept what is happening to this earthly body.

My Warrior is receiving foreign cells into their body, similar to welcoming strangers into one's home. Be near as the door opens to this unknown course.

Prepare my Warrior for the upcoming journey, and deliver strength for whatever destiny is Your will.

Bestow Your strength to accept what cannot be changed, the courage to change what can be, and the wisdom to know the difference.

Amen.

May Your arms bring comfort . . .

I consider that our present sufferings are not worth comparing with the glory that will be revealed in us.

ROMANS 8:18

LET THY WILL BE DONE

Teacher Most High,

In Your all-knowing love, You allowed cancer upon
_____. I ask for Your help now in teaching to accept
this undesirable and fearful path.

Show my Warrior how to believe in the words "Let Thy
will be done."

Shine Your light to guide the way. Shower Your wisdom
as all try to understand what is happening. Walk beside my
Warrior as each morning brings a new day. Bring forward
acceptance when traveling this course.

May the love and support from family, friends, medical
experts, and religious orders pour over my Warrior. Supply
what is necessary to practice self-care when feeling tired,
overwhelmed, discouraged, or scared. Give strength to calm
the troubled waters of our fearful souls.

Wrap Your arms around the heart and mind of Your
obedient student. Teach my Warrior and all of us to live by
Your commands and to trust in Your ways.

Let Thy will be done.

Amen.

May Your will be done ...

_____

_____

_____

_____

_____

_____

_____

_____

_____

_____

_____

_____

_____

"This, then, is how you should pray: 'Our Father in heaven,
hallowed be your name, your kingdom come, your will be done,
on earth as it is in heaven. Give us today our daily bread.
And forgive us our debts, as we also have forgiven our debtors.
And lead us not into temptation, but deliver us from the evil one.'"

MATTHEW 6:9–13

WOE BE THE PARENT

Lord of all,

Woe is the parent with a child in their arms that You have called upon to enter Your home.

As a baby is rocked, a child is hugged, or a young adult is comforted and held, I lift up _____, who fears missing precious many moments with this child.

Not only is this a loss of a parent to child, but also the child to parent.

Pour Your spiritual strength over this child.

Bless them with Your graces to continue to be developed and nurtured by loved ones left behind.

Lord of all, please extend Your arms to both parent and child. Give them strength, courage, and belief in Your eternal love as You become their place of peace.

Amen.

For the parent and child ...

_____
_____
_____
_____
_____
_____
_____
_____
_____
_____
_____
_____
_____
_____

"Come to me, all you who are weary and burdened, and I will give you rest. Take my yoke upon you and learn from me, for I am gentle and humble in heart, and you will find rest for your souls."

MATTHEW 11:28–29

BROKEN GLASS

King of Kings!

As I process the recent news, sadness and disbelief overwhelm me. I'm weak and broken, overcome with so many emotions.

I'm angry.

I want to scream and let the tears flow.

Instead, I bring You my Warrior.

Our once-clear picture of life has been shattered. How do we begin putting the pieces back together?

Be with us, mighty King, as we ask Your help in mending the damage caused by sickness and suffering.

Let Your strong hands unite us in prayer.

May Your healing presence be in our hearts, in our homes, and in _____'s body.

King of Kings, wrap Your arms tightly around my Warrior. Open our hearts to the work of Your hands so that we may know the power of Your eternal love. Instill in us a spirit of unity while repairing the brokenness.

Gather in me the strength to share Your glory. And, Heavenly Father, give us the courage to let Your will be done. Thank You, our King, our Lord.

Amen.

Repair the broken ...

Therefore we do not lose heart. Though outwardly we are
wasting away, yet inwardly we are being renewed day by
day. For our light and momentary troubles are achieving
for us an eternal glory that far outweighs them all. So we
fix our eyes not on what is seen, but on what is unseen, since
what is seen is temporary, but what is unseen is eternal.

2 CORINTHIANS 4:16–18

GIVING SPACE

Risen Lord,

It seems my Warrior has shut down, closed all lines of communication, and begun avoiding questions, discussion, and contact.

I pray my Warrior is speaking to You.

May I remember the importance of allowing my Warrior time, distance, and silence to process feelings and realities.

Please fill empty spaces in _____'s heart and mind.

Listen closely to silent pleas for mercy.

I know that you do not need to be told of my Warrior's need for You. I know that no matter the time or season, in joy and in sorrow, You are always present in our lives. There's no space from You, my Lord and my God.

Risen Lord, embed the words from Isaiah 41:10 — "So do not fear, I am with you; do not be dismayed for I am your God" — within hearts.

Amen.

May Your words fill empty spaces ...

"So do not fear, for I am with you; do not
be dismayed, for I am your God."

ISAIAH 41:10

MY PRAYER WEAPON

Lord, my Leader,

I call upon Your name as my shield and stronghold. I call upon the name of your Blessed Mother, Mary, who understands suffering and tragedy and loss.

In fighting the battle against _____'s diagnosis, prayer beads have become my weapon of choice against the enemy who seeks to control with fear, anger, and hate.

This holy instrument lies in the palm of our hands, providing a tactile sensation that builds in us the confidence and strength necessary to fight this earthly battle.

Through these beads, we lay our fervent prayers at Your feet. How could a son deny his mother's request?

Lord, my Leader, thank you for this powerful weapon of these beads, employed as protection against evils that attack the minds, bodies and souls of mankind. May You heed the prayers and petitions we ask of You through Your Mother, and protect your Warrior throughout this battle.

Amen.

Share your weapon . . .

_____

_____

_____

_____

_____

_____

_____

_____

_____

_____

_____

_____

_____

_____

_____

*Is anyone among you suffering? Let him pray. Is anyone
cheerful? Let him sing praise. Is anyone among you sick?
Let him call for the elders of the church, and let them pray
over him, anointing him with oil in the name of the Lord.*

JAMES 5:13–14 ESV

your COLLECTION:

PERSONAL PRAYERS, PETITIONS & MIRACLES

"*Prayer is not asking. Prayer is putting oneself in the hands of God, at His disposition, and listening to His voice in the depth of our hearts.*"

—*Mother Teresa*

SACRED SPACE

Since I began writing this book two years ago, the news of cancer entering (or re-entering) the lives of people I love has been heartbreaking. At times this news would leave me questioning these words written. And then I'd receive a call or a text: "My friend was diagnosed with cancer, I don't know what to do, is your book available yet?" or "My dad has cancer. It is stage 4, and I am scared. Can I read the words you wrote?"

These messages reminded me to continue this work. Still, I felt that this book would never be complete because there would always be more prayers to write. I could spend years trying to perfect this collection of prayers and petitions for your Warrior. A Word doc on my laptop doesn't serve anyone if it's not shared.

The following pages are your sacred space. Use them to journal your prayers and petitions, as well as the miracles you witness of God's grace, goodness, and love. Keep your heart, mind, and eyes open; I promise you will find them.

My prayers and petitions ...

Because you are my help, I sing in the shadow of your wings.

PSALM 63:7

Witnessing Gods miracles ...

_____

_____

_____

_____

_____

_____

_____

_____

_____

_____

_____

_____

_____

_____

_____

_____

_____

_____

The Lord will fight for you; you need to only be still.

EXODUS 14:14

Notes.

Notes.

EPILOGUE

Dear reader,

I hope this small book has helped bring you and your Warrior a bit of comfort, strength, and peace. As I stated at the beginning, this wasn't a book I wanted to write. Yet, it was something I believe we needed.

I couldn't pack this book with promises that reading these prayers will heal your Warrior. You and I both know that would be a lie.

While I don't know how your Warrior's story has turned out, I do believe God's love, goodness, strength, peace, and grace has been bestowed upon you and your Warrior during this journey.

I wish this wasn't a book I was called to write, yet I am honored and humbled to share this with you. May you never forget, your prayers and petitions matter.

In peace and gratitude,

Yvette

Made in the USA
Middletown, DE
23 September 2021

48283200R00060